DISCOVERING OUR HERITAGE

MEXICO

A GOLDEN PAST, A HOPEFUL FUTURE

BY R. CONRAD STEIN

DILLON PRESS
PARSIPPANY, NEW JERSEY

Photo Credits
Front Cover: Map, Ortelius Design; *l.* Sipa Press/Tor England; *m.* Charmayne McGee; *r.* Mexico Transcolor.
Allsport Photography/Simon Bruty: 85. The Bettmann Archive/Enzio Petersen: 104. Focus on Sports: 103. The Granger Collection: 44. Charmayne McGee: 22, 54, 65, 72, 93. Mexico Transcolor: 8, 15, 28, 37, 41, 89. Odyssey/Robert Frerck: 19. SBG: 111. Sipa Press/Tor England: 11. R. Conrad Stein: 9, 66, 74, 77, 78, 86. Superstock: 25. Sygma Photo News/Bill Naton: 102. Don Wolf: 33, 56, 60, 63. Map, Ortelius Design: 6.

Library of Congress Cataloging-in-Publication Data
Stein, R. Conrad.
    Mexico—a golden past, a hopeful future / by R. Conrad Stein.—
    1st ed.
    p. cm.—(Discovering our heritage)
    Includes bibliographical references and index.
    ISBN 0-87518-646-7 (Hardcover).—ISBN 0-382-39291-4 (pbk.)
    [1. Surveys the geography, history, people, folklore, family life,
education, sports, and culture of Mexico. Also includes a chapter on
Mexican Americans. 2. Mexico—Juvenile literature. 3. Mexico.]
    I. Title. II. Series.
    F1208.5S74 1997
    972—dc20   95-42578

 Published by Dillon Press
A Division of Simon & Schuster
299 Jefferson Road, Parsippany, NJ 07054

First edition
Printed in the United States of America
10 9 8 7 6 5 4 3 2 1

CONTENTS

Fast Facts About Mexico

Official Name: *Estados Unidos Mexicanos*, or United Mexican States.

Capital: Mexico City.

Location: North America, south of the United States of America. The Central American countries of Guatemala and Belize lie south and east of Mexico.

Area: Including its outlying islands, Mexico covers 761,600 square miles (1,972,544 square kilometers). *Greatest distances:* north to south, 1,250 miles (2,012 kilometers); east to west, 1,900 miles (3,060 kilometers). Mexico has 6,320 miles (10,170 kilometers) of coastline.

Elevation: *Highest*—Mount Orizaba, 18,701 feet (5,700 meters) above sea level. *Lowest*—33 feet (10 meters) below sea level, near the city of Mexicali.

Population: 94,545,000 (1993 estimated). *Distribution*— about 75 percent urban; 25 percent rural. In the 1970s and 1980s, Mexican cities experienced explosive growth.

Government: Mexico is divided into 31 states and 1 federal district. Its national government is headed by a president who is elected to a six-year term. Mexico's government also includes a legislature made up of two houses: the 64-member Senate and the Chamber of Deputies, numbering about 200 members.

Important Products: *Manufacturing*—cars and car parts, iron and steel, food products. *Agriculture*—corn, beef cattle, wheat, coffee. *Mining*—petroleum, natural gas, iron ore, silver.

Unit of Money: Peso. In 1995 the rate of exchange for the New Peso (NP) was about five pesos to one U.S. dollar. See Appendix Three for more information about Mexican currency.

Official Language: Spanish. Indian languages such as Maya or Nahuatl (once spoken by the Aztecs) are still in use, but today practically every Mexican speaks Spanish.

Religions: More than 90 percent of Mexicans are Roman Catholics. The constitution guarantees religious freedom, and there are also non-Catholic churches in many big cities.

Flag: Three vertical stripes of green, white, and red. The green stripe stands for independence, the white stripe stands for religion, and the red stripe for the unity of the Mexican people. In the center (the white stripe) is a picture of an eagle perched on a cactus and eating a snake—a reference to the Aztec legend. This picture is a version of the Mexican coat of arms.

National Anthem: The National Hymn of Mexico (*Himno Nacional de Mexico*), a lively song that urges Mexicans to answer the battle cry.

Special Holidays: February 5 (Constitution Day), March 21 (Birthday of President Benito Juárez), May 5 (anniversary of the battle of Puebla), September 16 (Independence Day), October 12 (Columbus Day or Day of the Race), November 2 (Day of the Dead), December 12 (Day of Our Lady of Guadalupe).

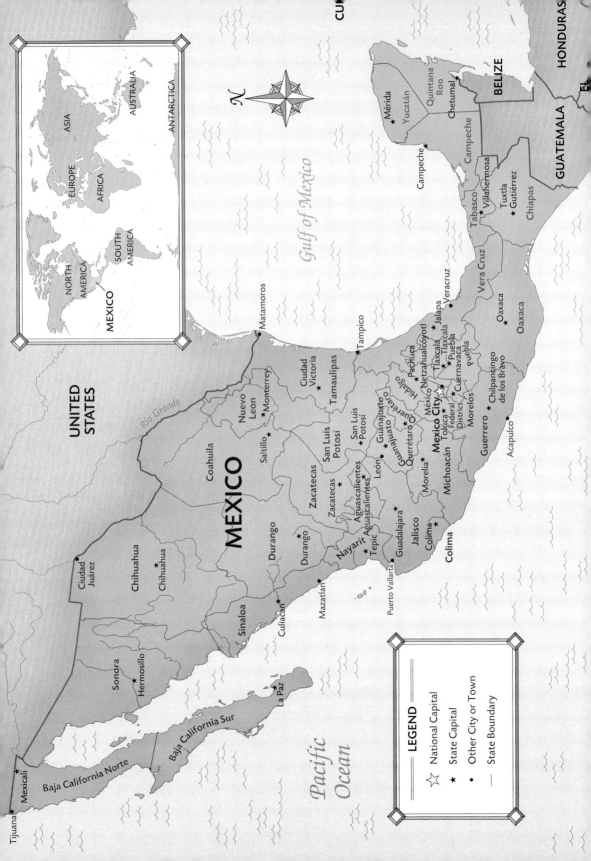

AN EXCITING LAND

Juan is a *tragafuego*, a fire-eater. He is a thin teenager who roams the streets of Mexico City carrying a plastic container filled with kerosene and a torch made from a bent coat hanger with a cloth wrapped around its tip. At twilight he dips the torch in the kerosene, lights it with a cigarette lighter, and holds it, flaming, above his head. A crowd gathers to watch the show. Juan takes a mouthful of kerosene. Then he holds the lighted torch inches from his mouth and, with a loud whoosh, blows the kerosene through the flame and into the evening sky. A finger of fire, 15 or 20 feet (4.5 or 6 meters) long, shoots out of his mouth. Spectators feel the blast of heat and gasp.

After his act, Juan passes a coffee can around the crowd, hoping to collect a few coins. If the onlookers think his performance is better than that of the other fire-eaters who work the streets, they might tip him well. But competition is fierce. Some of the tragafuegos paint their faces green and white to add to the spectacle.

Juan is destroying his lungs, dying a slow death to make a living in Mexico City. Decent jobs are scarce in the Mexican capital. Many people resort to street entertainment to earn money. Fortunately, most other entertainers choose less dangerous acts than fire-eating.

A view of Mexico City

On one corner, a short, thin man wears an old-fashioned tuxedo and a top hat and carries a cane. He walks stiff-legged and twirls the cane as if it were a baton. Then he dances to unheard music. He is a very talented imitator of the silent-screen star Charlie Chaplin.

Nearby, a two-man comedy team begins its act. One wears a bonnet, like one worn by a baby, and asks simple–minded questions of his older, wiser partner. Their act features clownlike falls and sneak kicks in the seat of the pants. Neither comedian is a great talent. Their jokes are extremely corny.

Many people in Mexico City are forced to make their living doing marginal jobs such as shining shoes.

"I bought some pills at the market yesterday that were supposed to improve my memory," says the wise one.

"Oh yeah? Did the pills work?" asks the baby.

"I don't know. I forgot to take them."

The lively world of street entertainment is a fascinating aspect of Mexico City life. The big city can be harsh, even cruel, but it is also an amazing place. Mexico City is the heart and soul of Mexico—one of the most exciting countries on earth.

Mexico and the United States—Neighbors Apart

"Mexico, so far from God, so close to the United States" runs an old Mexican saying. Mexico, a struggling newly industrialized nation, lies just to the south of the United States, the world's most prosperous nation. Though physically close as neighbors, the two countries could not be further apart in other ways.

As might be expected, all kinds of opportunities in the United States lure Mexicans north. A steady stream of Mexicans, seeking better wages and living conditions, crosses the border between the two countries. Some enter the United States with proper immigration documents, but many cross the border illegally. It is estimated that of the 3 to 6 million people living and working illegally in the United States, over half are Mexicans.

Mexico's other neighbors, to the south and east, are the Central American countries of Guatemala and Belize. Mexico is prosperous by comparison with most nations in Central America. In an unexpected twist, the Mexican government has a problem with Central American workers crossing the border illegally to earn better wages in Mexican factories.

A Land of Mighty Mountains

A story 450 years old tells of a day when the king of

Rugged mountains cover large areas of Mexico.

Spain summoned to his court Hernán Cortés, who had recently explored and conquered Mexico.

"What does the new land of Mexico look like?" asked the king. Cortés pointed to the ceiling. Then he spread his arms. The king sat, impatient and fidgeting. Finally Cortés grabbed a sheet of paper from a scribe. He folded it, crushed it into a jagged ball, and held it out before the king.

"There, Your Majesty," he said. "This is how Mexico looks."

Mexico is a land of mountains that rise from the sea like giant teeth. Two jagged mountain ranges—the Sierra Madre East and the Sierra Madre West—hug Mexico's coasts and sweep the length of the country. Between the two mountain ranges spreads a broad plateau. Even the plateau is mountainous, looking much like the crumpled-up piece of paper that Cortés held before the king.

Mountains determine the climate in Mexico. Many think of Mexico as a tropical country, with steaming-hot temperatures. They are wrong. The coastal areas tend to be hot, but the central plateau is temperate—not too hot, not too cold. People living there have to wear sweaters or jackets at night during the winter months. The climate at higher elevations is generally cool. In fact, many mountaintops in the region are covered with snow year-round. By contrast, deserts cover a large area of the northern plateau near the Mexico-U.S. border.

To the south the Yucatán Peninsula juts into the Gulf of Mexico. The Yucatán is one of the few areas in Mexico where mountains do not prevail. Thick jungle grows in the Yucatán and in the south near Mexico's border with Belize and Guatemala.

A Sometimes-Treacherous Land

September 19, 1985, dawned like any other day in

Mexico City. As the sun rose over the rooftops, smog was already beginning to settle on the capital. Then, at 7:18 in the morning, a deep rumbling sound startled the residents of the city. Trees and light posts did an eerie dance. Buildings swayed. Bricks, plaster, and shards of broken glass rained on the sidewalks.

Earthquake!

One man in a high-rise apartment building felt the floor suddenly sink underneath him. "It was like I was on an elevator," he said. In hundreds of buildings, roofs and floors collapsed inward, one on top of the other, burying the people inside. Some buildings shook so violently that their outer walls peeled off, leaving only naked steel skeletons standing. Underground pipes burst, sending up geysers of water. Dozens of fires broke out.

The 1985 earthquake lasted only a few seconds, but it was the greatest natural disaster in Mexican history. Some authorities estimate that as many as 20,000 people were killed. Thousands more were injured, and some 100,000 were made homeless. Still, the great tremor came as no surprise to the Mexican people. For years, scientists had predicted that the Mexico City region would be rocked by a powerful quake. And, scientists said, it could happen again any time.

Earthquakes have terrified Mexicans since ancient times. The most frequent and severe quakes tend to occur in a region south of Mexico City where the Sierra Madre East and the Sierra Madre West come together. This region has four times as many major earthquakes as the quake-prone state of California in the United States.

Volcanoes also threaten life in Mexico. Mexico has at least 3,000 volcanoes, many of which are active. One volcano blistered out of a cornfield in 1943, almost under the feet of a horrified farmer. Spewing smoke and lava, the volcano grew to a height of 1,700 feet (518 meters) before it became inactive.

Mexico's mountain scenery is spectacular. Like waves on an endless sea, one mountain range follows another into the horizon. The mountain air, away from the cities, is as pure as any air on earth. But this overwhelming natural beauty rests on treacherous land. Volcanic eruptions and earthquakes strike with little or no warning. As one Mexico City newspaper observed recently, "Mexico is sitting on a time bomb."

Mexican Cities

At the turn of the century, less than 10 percent of Mexicans lived in cities. Today nearly 80 percent are city dwellers. The greatest number of people moved from farms to cities during the 1970s and 1980s. In that period, crop prices dropped, driving small farmers off the land, and large

Street scene in Monterrey, Mexico

farmers invested in harvesting machinery that reduced their need for farm workers. Because they could no longer make a living in the rural areas, millions of Mexicans flocked to the cities, seeking work. Old cities burst their boundaries, and new cities grew out of nothing.

The city with the tongue-twisting Aztec name Netzahualcóyotl is just one example of the explosive growth in Mexican urban areas. "Netza," as its residents call it, is located near Mexico City's airport. Before 1960 the place was a barren landscape of cactus, rocks, and swirling desert sands. Then immigrants from the farms began to arrive. The newcomers came so fast that they were

called parachutists, because they seemed almost to drop
from the sky. They built shacks of scrap brick and
corrugated tin or cans pounded flat for roofing. Today
Netzahualcóyotl is home to more than 3 million people
and is Mexico's second largest city.

The population of greater Mexico City is more
than 20 million. An accurate census is difficult to take in
the capital because the city's boundaries continue to expand.
Many population experts believe Mexico City has
overtaken Tokyo, Japan, as the most populated city in the
world. As new residents flooded in, Mexico City enveloped
surrounding cornfields and cow pastures. The majority of
new people were poor and built shacks similar to those
in Netzahualcóyotl. Mexico City residents call the
neighborhoods of shacks *ciudades perdidas*, "lost cities."

Historically the central plateau has held the bulk of
Mexico's population. All five of Mexico's largest cities
are located there. Beginning with the largest, Mexico's
most populated cities are Mexico City, Netzahualcóyotl,
Guadalajara, Monterrey, and Ciudad Juárez. Each
experienced remarkable growth in the 1970s and 1980s.

Industry and the Quest for Jobs

Mexico is an ancient land, but its people are young. In
1991, Mexico's population stood at 90,379,000. More than

half the people were under the age of 20. Each year, more than a million young people leave school and begin to search for jobs. Only about one third of the young job seekers find full-time employment. Over the years, Mexico has developed large industries, but its economy simply cannot accommodate all the new workers entering the job market. As a result, unemployment is high. Millions of Mexicans hold low-paying jobs with little future, such as selling newspapers and candy or performing as entertainers on the streets.

Oil was once considered to be the "black gold" that would lift Mexico out of poverty. Mexico is the world's fourth largest oil producer. The nation has estimated oil reserves (oil still in the ground) that match those of the oil-producing giant Saudi Arabia. But the drilling and refining of oil do not generate a large number of jobs. In addition, when the world price of oil dropped dramatically in the 1980s, profits fell. So the resource once thought of as Mexico's black gold has lost its glitter in recent years.

Manufacturing in Mexico offers more job opportunities than does the oil industry. In the 1970s and 1980s huge factories were built near the U.S. border to make automobile engines, electric motors, radios and televisions, computers, furniture, and kitchen appliances. Most of these factories, called *maquiladoras,* are owned by companies in the United States. The U.S. owners of the maquiladoras employ

Mexican workers in the factories and pay them lower wages than U.S. workers would accept. By 1993 more than 2,200 maquiladoras had been built. They employ some 500,000 Mexicans. The Mexican government welcomes the factories because they provide work for the many Mexicans seeking jobs. But workers on both sides of the border complain about the maquiladoras. In the 1990s the average pay for a maquiladora worker was less than $1 an hour. For the same work a factory hand in the United States earned $6 an hour.

Mexico's economic relationship with the United States changed in 1994 with the enactment of the North American Free Trade Agreement (NAFTA). The aim of the agreement is to cut tariffs, or taxes on goods, and to create a free-trade zone between Canada, the United States, and Mexico. Although NAFTA was finally approved by the U.S. Congress, it was opposed by many, including labor unions in the United States. The unions claimed U.S. factory jobs would be lost to lower-paid Mexican workers. Those in favor of NAFTA, including U.S. President Bill Clinton, believed free trade under the terms of the agreement would promote prosperity in all three countries.

Besides oil production and manufacturing, tourism is a major industry in Mexico. The country has attractive beach resorts such as Acapulco, Manzanillo, Cozumel, and Cancún. On the Yucatán Peninsula stand ancient ruins

Mexico's beautiful beach resorts, such as this one in Cancún, attract many tourists.

from Mexico's Maya civilization. Inland are the lovely colonial villages of San Miguel de Allende, Guanajuato, and Taxco. To enjoy all these delights, six million tourists visit Mexico each year and spend about $3 billion. Tourism creates thousands of jobs for Mexicans in hotels, restaurants, and shops.

Government

Mexico is officially known as the *Estados Unidos Mexicanos*, the United Mexican States. Like its northern neighbor, it is divided into states that are responsible for local government. Mexico has 31 states and 1 federal district. The federal district includes Mexico City. Mexico's national government is led by a president and a legislature. The legislature is made up of two houses—the Senate and the Chamber of Deputies. The country's constitution, written in 1917 at the height of revolutionary war, gives Mexico's president great power. The president appoints all cabinet members, and the cabinet has a large say in running public works. The president is elected to a six-year term and cannot be reelected. All Mexican citizens age 18 and over are allowed to vote.

Mexico's leading political party is the *Partido Revolucionario Institucional* (Institutional Revolutionary Party), or PRI. Until recently, Mexico was a one-party country. The PRI won all major elections. In fact, the government and the party were largely one and the same. But in the 1980s, rival parties began cutting into the PRI's power. In 1988 an opposition party almost defeated Carlos Salinas de Gortari, the PRI's candidate for president. Mexico's movement away from one-party rule is feared by some observers who believe it could lead to instability. The development of political parties is praised by others who see it as a healthy demand on the part of the Mexican people for greater democracy.

Political change has created turmoil in Mexico in recent years. On New Year's Day in 1994, Indian people in the southern state of Chiapas led a revolt against the government. Chiapas is the poorest of all Mexican states. The Indians demanded better roads and fairer land distribution in their region. For twelve days, fighting raged in Chiapas. More than 145 people were killed before order was finally restored. A few months later, the leading presidential candidate, Luis Donaldo Colosio, was shot in the head and killed by a gunman. The PRI named a new leader, Ernesto Zedillo, to replace Colosio. Many people predicted that riots and other forms of violence would rock the country when elections were held in August. But the elections were peaceful. Zedillo won, and the PRI held onto the presidency as it had without interruption since the party's founding in 1929. At his victory celebration Zedillo said, "We are facing a historic opportunity to create a government for the common good in which the interests of all are recognized."

*The many faces of Mexico are shown here as students salute the flag
and sing the Mexican national anthem.*

THE MEXICAN PEOPLE

Three races make up the bulk of the population of Mexico—mestizos, Indians, and whites. The exact population breakdown among the three groups is difficult to determine, since the government stopped using racial categories in its 1920 census. The majority of Mexicans are mestizos. The mestizo race is the result of intermarriage between Indians and European whites.

No one agrees on how to define members of the Indian race. Today's Indians are descendants of Mexico's original people, those who occupied the land before whites arrived. In Mexico, being Indian is almost a state of mind. An Indian is thought of as a person who uses Indian expressions in speech and who lives in a village where the people identify themselves as Indians. Generally, Indians are the most impoverished group in Mexican society. To the Mexican mind, an Indian who acquires wealth and adopts citified ways suddenly gains a different identity. Such a newly rich person might very well whisper to friends, "You know, I used to be an Indian."

Whites are the smallest group, after mestizos and Indians. The whites in Mexico are descendants of Europeans, mostly Spaniards, who have been immigrating to Mexico for almost 500 years. Small numbers of blacks and Asians also live in the country.

Whether they are mestizos, Indians, or whites, nine out of ten Mexicans claim to be Roman Catholics. No law makes Catholicism the official religion, and freedom of religion is guaranteed by the nation's constitution. Still, Mexico is staunchly Catholic. Mexicans cling to the Church and tend to be devout in religious practices. It is common for Mexican people to stop and make the Sign of the Cross when passing a church. On the front door of many houses is a sign that proudly proclaims *Este hogar es católico* ("This household is Catholic").

Practically all Mexicans speak Spanish. In fact, many Spanish professors claim that Mexicans speak the purest form of the language, purer even than that spoken in Spain. Until the 1940s, people in isolated rural communities spoke only Indian languages. Today it is estimated that less than 7 percent of the people still use the Indian languages that were once so common.

A Passion for the Arts

Mexicans are creative people who express themselves in many ways. Mexico's murals, or wall paintings, are its crowning art form. In the 1920s, three great muralists— Diego Rivera, José Orozco, and David Siqueiros— astounded the artistic world with their sweeping scenes and

This detail from a Diego Rivera mural depicts the Spanish conquest.

brilliant colors. Diego Rivera was the most famous muralist of the "Big Three." One of Rivera's beloved murals is painted on the walls of the government headquarters building in Mexico City's central plaza. The mural offers the artist's interpretation of Mexican history. On the left-hand side, Rivera has painted scenes of pre-Columbian Indians living in an idyllic society. Then he portrays brutal Spaniards arriving and enslaving the Indians. Finally, Rivera depicts a glorious revolution against Spain and against all of Mexico's oppressors.

In sharp contrast to the artists, Mexican writers of the twentieth century often present a grim picture of Mexican life. In his book *The Death of Artemio Cruz*, Carlos Fuentes tells of a powerful but corrupt landowner who gleefully tramples on the rights of his employees and his business competitors. Author Juan Rulfo's books *The Burning Plain* and *Pedro Páramo* present a similar theme, describing the struggles of farmers trying to grow crops on Mexico's rocky, dry land. Standing over his farm, one of Rulfo's characters says, "Nothing will rise from this stony soil, not even vultures."

The novelist, poet, and philosopher Octavio Paz is justly called the dean of Mexican writers. In 1990, Paz won the Nobel Prize for Literature. Paz's famous book, *The Labyrinth of Solitude*, puzzles over the Mexican character, in particular the people's mix of Spanish and Indian bloodlines. Paz observes, "The Mexican does not want to be either an Indian or a Spaniard. Nor does he want to be descended from them. He denies them. . . . He becomes the son of Nothingness. His beginnings are his own self."

Wherever you go in Mexico, you are bound to find a man or a woman selling carved wooden statues, delicate silver jewelry, tiny figures fashioned out of wire, or pottery painted with blazing colors. Most of these items are not mass produced at a factory. Instead they are carefully created in a home workshop by a craftsperson who is highly skilled at his or her work. Mexican handicrafts are world famous. Carved figures and pieces of jewelry made in Mexico years ago are now displayed in museums. Items crafted today are sold at special stands in the markets. In Mexico City there are large stores devoted exclusively to selling items made in the countryside. In those stores, foreign tourists and Mexicans alike browse through a delightful assortment of figurines and pottery pieces hoping to find that one perfect item they have always wanted to put above the fireplace back home.

Think of Mexican music, and a loud and brassy mariachi band comes immediately to mind. A typical mariachi group features seven musicians—a singer, two horn players, two violinists, and two guitarists. Band members wear dark uniforms, usually decorated with sparkling silver ornaments. On their heads they wear broad-rimmed hats. It is said that mariachi music began in the 1860s, when French troops briefly occupied Mexico and hired bands to play whenever one of their soldiers married a Mexican woman. Emotion rules the mariachi band. The singer, who is usually the group's leader, wails out, "Ay-ay-ay-ay!" whenever the song takes a sad twist. Tears will flow from the eyes of a singer who is particularly devoted to his work.

Folk music and folk dancing are honored throughout the land. The country's famous folk-dance troupe, Bailes

Folk dancers give a lively performance.

Folklóricos, has thrilled audiences in every part of the world. In northern Mexico, where cattle ranching is the way of life, high-spirited ranchero music is a passion. This music can be compared to the country and western music that is so popular in the United States. Ranchero music originated with the lonesome cowboy working the plains at night. The leader of a ranchero group plays one of the strangest instruments in any band: a piece of wood. Wired to the leader's belt is a sawed-off piece of two-by-four that he taps with drumsticks while the rest of the band accompanies him with accordians and guitar.

Country Life and Village Life

Well before dawn the mother of a typical farm family pats ground corn into thin, pancake-shaped tortillas for the family's breakfast. Tortillas are the common bread of Mexico. No meal is complete without a stack of them, served piping hot.

After a breakfast of tortillas, beans, and coffee, the farm family heads out to the fields to begin work. A fortunate farmer who has well-watered and fertile land will grow crops such as cucumbers, strawberries, tomatoes, and bell peppers, which can be sold for cash. But most Mexican land is rocky and starved for rain. It can support only corn, which is a particularly rugged crop.

The vast majority of Mexican farms lie on the central plateau, where soils are adequate but rainfall spotty. The rainy season in the central plateau usually begins in June. If the rains come late, entire villages, led by their priests, march to the fields to pray for showers to begin. If the rains have not started by July, the villagers take statues of the Christ child or the Virgin Mary out of the church and implore them to command the clouds to do their work. Old farmers might secretly pray to Tlaloc, the ancient Aztec god of rainfall.

On Sundays, farm people journey to the village to attend church and enjoy a day of rest. A trip to the village also means a visit to the village market. Markets in rural towns are a madcap blend of colors, smells, and sounds. Most village markets consist of 20 or more stalls situated in a square, each stall covered by canvas. Food sellers display their goods in little pyramids—a pyramid of tomatoes, a pyramid of oranges, and so on. Ancient paintings by Aztec and Maya artists show vendors presenting their goods in exactly the same manner. Every village market has an *herbero*, an herb seller. The herb seller places little signs over the bags of herbs for sale: "Good for Sleeplessness," "Will Help a Poor Appetite," "For High Blood Pressure."

More than a place to buy goods, the village market is also an open-air forum. It is where farmers and townspeople meet to chat, joke, and gossip. But, of course, shopping is the major purpose of most people who come to the markets. Bargaining is expected. "How much for that pair of socks?" asks a customer. "Ayyyy, too expensive," says the customer and pretends to walk away. Invariably the vendor will call the customer back and offer a lower price. The give-and-take is usually good-natured. "You're robbing me," says the seller. "But go ahead, take the socks, it's Sunday."

On Sunday nights, people gather at the town's central square. In most villages a church towers over one end of the central plaza, and the city hall stands at the other end. The square has benches, shade trees, and walkways. In the cool of the evening the *paseos*, or informal walks, begin. Hundreds of people walk in rings around and around the plaza. Years ago, paseo tradition demanded that boys walk clockwise around the plaza, and girls walk counterclockwise. Now and then they would giggle at one another. These days the paseo has no such rules, but it still offers a marvelous opportunity for boys and girls to flirt.

Many Mexicos

In Mexico, one can hear regional differences in music and taste them in the food. Mexicans claim they can also see regional characteristics in people's faces and behavior.

People from northern Mexico walk at a faster pace than people from the south, for instance. Regionalism is a lively, vibrant force in the nation. There always have been, and continue to be, many Mexicos.

As most people do, Mexicans create stereotypes, or generalizations, about the behavior of others. For example, they claim people from the city of Monterrey have no sense of humor and are tightfisted with money. Is this true, or is it simply a stereotype? Mexicans will argue the point endlessly. And the generalizations go on and on: The people of Veracruz live too much for pleasure and spend money foolishly; residents of Puebla are the most religious of all Mexicans; Jalisco dwellers are the best cooks; those from the Yucatán are simple country folk who are often the object of jokes.

One of Mexico's fastest-growing regions stretches along its 2,000-mile (3,218-kilometer) border with the United States. There two cultures meet and blend together. Children living in the border region learn English by watching American cartoons broadcast from the United States. Signs in English advertise "snack bars" or "parking lots" instead of using the equivalent Spanish words. Dollars are exchanged freely with pesos. Most people who live on the border—*la frontera*—have visited the United States several times, although few have ever been to Mexico City.

Young shoppers rest at the market in the southern state of Chiapas.

The Mexico City region has a powerful influence on national life. The most important television stations and movie companies all have their headquarters in the capital. Opinion makers such as journalists, novelists, and leading college professors are invariably from the big city. Yet, Mexico City dwellers are often unpopular in nearby towns.

On weekends wealthy Mexico City men and women flock to their getaway homes in small towns to escape the capital's smog. The local people claim the Mexico City residents are rude to waiters and short-tempered with maids. A person from Mexico City is called a *chilango*, a term that cannot be translated easily. *Chilango* is not a swearword, but it is never considered to be complimentary.

The Legacy of Three Cultures

Near downtown Mexico City spreads a broad open area called the Plaza of Three Cultures. On one side of the plaza stand the ruins of an ancient pyramid; on another side rises a church built hundreds of years ago by the Spaniards; and towering over both structures is a glass and steel high-rise building. These buildings represent the three great cultural periods of Mexican history—Indian, Spanish, and modern. When Mexican schoolchildren learn about their nation's history, they study these three periods. Every day groups of schoolchildren wearing blue and white uniforms visit the Plaza of Three Cultures. There they gaze at the three buildings constructed hundreds of years apart, and they marvel at the very different cultures that have shaped the Mexican nation.

Ancient Mexico

Some 30,000 years ago, bands of hunters trekked out of Asia, crossed a land bridge that no longer exists, and entered the North American continent. Christopher Columbus later mistakenly referred to the descendants of these people as Indians. By 10,000 B.C. groups of these early peoples had drifted south and were hunting huge elephants called mammoths in the same valley where Mexico City sprawls today. As the centuries passed, the hunters learned to plant corn. A legend says that long ago the ants hid corn from human beings. But then a god miraculously turned himself into an ant, entered an anthill, and brought back a kernel of corn to present to human farmers.

The first monumental civilization to rise in Mexico was that of a mysterious people called the Olmecs. The Olmecs lived along the Gulf of Mexico coast in the present-day state of Veracruz. Beginning in 1200 B.C. they constructed earthen mounds and stone pyramids. They also carved heads out of boulders. Some of the boulders weighed 40 tons (36 metric tons). The Olmec heads have frozen stares and are covered by tight-fitting caps that look strangely like football helmets. Surprisingly, the faces have features similar to those of black Africans. This detail has led some scholars to speculate that the Olmecs had contact with Africa. The sculptures show remarkable artistic skill, but to this day their significance is a mystery.

About A.D. 250, another people known as the Mayas began building an amazing society in what is now southern Mexico, Guatemala, and Honduras. The Mayas were the scholars of ancient America. Fascinated by the movements of the planets and stars, Maya astronomers plotted the course of the planet Jupiter with extraordinary precision.

The pyramids at Teotihuacán were built by a mysterious ancient culture. They stand near Mexico City and now serve as a tourist attraction.

The calendar used by Maya priests was one of the most accurate developed in ancient times. Visitors today stare in awe at the dome-shaped observatory in the ruined city of Chichén Itzá that Maya engineers built hundreds of years ago.

At the same time that the Maya civilization was thriving, another culture built a massive pyramid complex some 30 miles (48 kilometers) south of present-day Mexico City. No one knows the name of the people who built the pyramid complex, but the ancient Aztec peoples were astounded when they first saw the structures. The Aztecs concluded that they had been built by gods, because certainly no mere mortals could erect such mighty pyramids. For this reason the Aztecs named the city Teotihuacán, "where men become gods." The huge pyramids of Teotihuacán still stand. Today they are a popular tourist attraction, and thousands come each year to wonder at this ancient site.

The Aztecs came from the north in the 1300s, searching for the fulfillment of a legendary promise. Decades earlier their priests claimed that a god commanded them to build a capital city in a place where they saw an eagle perched on a cactus, devouring a snake. The god also prophesied that the Aztecs would soon command a great nation. After years of wandering, the Aztecs finally saw the eagle, the snake, and the cactus on an island in the middle of a large lake. There, in 1325, they built the greatest city in North America. They called their capital Tenochtitlán. At the height of the Aztec Empire, Tenochtitlán, which was constructed where Mexico City stands today, contained 60,000 houses, dozens of tall pyramids, a castle for the ruler, and even a royal zoo. The city was so fantastic that when travelers from Spain first saw it, many thought they were dreaming.

New Spain

In 1519 a band of 500 Spanish warriors splashed onto Mexican shores at what is now the city of Veracruz. The Spaniards were led by an ambitious captain named Hernán Cortés, who sought gold for himself and new lands for his king. The coastal people told Cortés that vast amounts of gold could be found inland at the Aztec capital. The people along the coast called the capital Mexico. Without hesitation, Cortés and his men marched toward the heart of the Aztec Empire.

As he advanced, Cortés learned that Aztecs were hated by their neighbors. The Aztec people were passionate believers in human sacrifice—the ritualistic killing of men and women to win the favor of their gods. In their quest for sacrificial victims they entered surrounding cities and carried off men and women to be slaughtered on their altars. Because Aztec power was resented by so many, Cortés was able to gather thousands of Indian allies. In 1521 the Spaniards made a crushing attack on the Aztec capital, destroyed the city, and conquered the once mighty Aztec Empire. With the fall of the Aztecs, the land now belonged to the invaders from Europe. Cortés named the land New Spain.

After Cortés's conquest of the Aztecs, thousands of Spaniards immigrated to New Spain. They brought European crops with them, including citrus fruit and wheat. They introduced wheeled vehicles and draft animals such as the burro. In the years to come, it would be impossible to imagine Mexico without the ever-present burro. But the Spaniards also unwittingly brought diseases with them. Among the diseases they introduced were measles and smallpox. The Indians had no immunity against these diseases, and the new sicknesses severely reduced the native population. At the time of Cortés's arrival, more than 10 million and perhaps as many as 25 million native people lived in Mexico. By 1700, only 1 million Indians remained.

Spanish settlers gave New Spain the Spanish language and the Catholic religion. Priests found the Indian people to be willing converts to the new religion, but many villages still worshipped statues of their ancient gods in secret. During the Spanish period, more than 12,000 churches were built. Towns grew around the church towers. The towns were graced with colonial architecture, a delightful blend of Old World techniques and New World materials. Today handsome villages such as San Miguel de Allende, Guanajuato, and Taxco are well-preserved masterpieces of the colonial tradition.

Under Spanish rule three distinct social classes—the whites, the mestizos, and the Indians—developed. The whites were the primary landowners and wielded the political power. The mestizos were granted a few privileges but still lived at a far lower status than the white ruling class. The Indians were treated as a conquered race and lived in poverty. Even after Mexico became independent from Spain, this rigid class system, based largely on race, continued.

For 300 years the flag of New Spain fluttered over its

The statue of Pipila in the city of Guanajuato. Pipila was a hero in the Mexican War of Independence against Spain.

capital, Mexico City. But by the 1800s the people of Mexico, especially the wealthy whites, had grown to resent foreign rule. On September 16, 1810, a mild-mannered, bookish priest named Father Miguel Hidalgo y Castillo called the villagers together in the churchyard of the town of Dolores. Instead of celebrating a mass, Hidalgo issued a cry for revolution. The cry sparked a ten-year war that finally ended Spain's rule over Mexico. Today, September 16 is celebrated as Mexican Independence Day, and the impassioned speech delivered by the priest is called the *Grito de Hidalgo*, the "Cry of Hidalgo."

Mexico the Nation

When Mexico won its independence it was a huge country, about twice its present size. Its northern boundary stretched well beyond the Rio Grande, embracing what are now the states of Texas, New Mexico, Arizona, and California, and parts of Nevada, Utah, and Colorado. These northern regions of Mexico were undeveloped. Few Mexicans lived in the north, and authorities in Mexico City had little control over the vast territory. To the north lay the young and ambitious American nation. As the United States expanded, its people coveted the fertile lands of northern Mexico.

The lands that are now Texas were Mexico's first loss. For years, farmers from the southern United States had been immigrating to Texas with the approval of the Mexican government. In 1835 these settlers rebelled against Mexico and declared Texas an independent nation. The Texas revolt was brutally crushed by the Mexican political and military leader Antonio de Santa Anna, who slaughtered the Texas defenders at the battle of the Alamo. Texas forces later regrouped to defeat Santa Anna.

The conflict over Texas strained relations between Mexico and the United States. The two countries went to war in 1846. Mexico, unprepared for war, was overwhelmed by the U.S. army. U.S. forces occupied much of Mexico, including Mexico City. In 1848, Mexican leaders were forced to sign the Treaty of Hidalgo, which ended the war. Terms of the treaty were harsh. Mexico gave up all of its northern lands to the United States. The loss of these lands hit Mexico especially hard when gold was discovered in California just a few months after the treaty was signed. Overnight, California became the richest region on the Pacific coast of North America. To this day, Mexicans are bitter over their enormous loss of territory following the 1846–1848 war with the United States.

In 1858, civil war broke out in Mexico. In the conflict, old-line government and church leaders opposed a new political movement that wanted change. The new movement was led by President Benito Juárez. Juárez was a Zapotec Indian who had been born into poverty. As president he championed the cause of Indians, and he promised to build schools throughout the countryside. But the new programs were abandoned when Mexico exploded into civil war. Because of the war, Mexico was unable to pay its debts, including debts to France. France used the debt issue as an excuse to send troops to Mexico. On May 5, 1862, the

*Benito Juárez served as president of Mexico from 1867
until his death in 1872.*

Mexican army soundly defeated a French force at the battle of Puebla. Mexicans still celebrate this victory in their *Cinco de mayo* ("Fifth of May") fiesta. But after the battle, France sent a larger army and installed a handpicked emperor, Ferdinand Maximilian, who ruled Mexico for three years. In 1867 Maximilian was overthrown and executed by forces loyal to Juárez. Juárez assumed the office of president but died in 1872 before his ambitious programs could be launched.

After Juárez's death a political strongman named Porfirio Díaz took power and headed the government for the next 30 years. Díaz believed it was his mission to industrialize Mexico. Under his leadership, factories were built, 9,000 miles (14,500 kilometers) of railroad track were laid down, and the output of mines tripled. But in pushing his country toward modernization, Díaz broke up labor unions and allowed the land owned by poor farmers to be gobbled up by plantation owners.

In 1910, rebellions broke out against Díaz's iron-fisted rule. In the north the rebels were led by Pancho Villa, a cattle rustler turned revolutionary. In the south the peasant leader Emiliano Zapata organized poor farmers into an efficient and deadly army. Díaz was forced to resign from office and flee the country. Momentary peace was restored when Francisco Madero was elected president in 1911. But a powerful spirit of revolution had taken hold in Mexico, and Madero was unable to keep the peace. In 1913 the crafty general Victoriano Huerta overthrew Madero and ordered him to be shot. A terrible civil war raged for the next seven years. Forces loyal to the rebels fought forces loyal to the government, and rival generals fought each other. During a ten-year span from 1910 to 1920, almost 2 million Mexicans died in the fighting. In terms of blood spilled, the Mexican Revolution of 1910 was the costliest war ever fought in the Americas, surpassing even the American Civil War.

When the fighting died down in 1920, Mexico arose from the ruins as a unified society for the first time in its history. Gone, at least officially, were the class distinctions between whites, mestizos, and Indians. Now all were Mexicans.

During World War II the U.S. government desperately needed workers. It established the bracero program, which allowed Mexican farm laborers to enter the United States with temporary work permits. After the war Mexicans continued to emigrate to the United States. The flight north intensified during the Mexican currency crises of the 1970s and 1980s, when the Mexican peso lost buying power. Many Mexican workers determined their currency was next to worthless and set off to the United States where they could earn dollars.

Some Modern Problems

"Too many cars, look at them all," said a Mexico City policeman as he desperately tried to direct traffic at a busy downtown intersection. "Let me tell you something—this city is in deep trouble." Behind the officer, buses, cars, and trucks—all part of a huge traffic jam—belched clouds of black smoke into the sky. Because of the fumes it was difficult to see the other side of the street. Such is a typical day in Mexico City.

The Mexican capital is situated in a bowl-shaped valley, ringed on all sides by mountains. The mountains prevent cleansing breezes from entering the city. Pollutants spewed from the capital's 3 million motor vehicles and 35,000 factories collect in a poisonous cloud that hangs over the city, day after smog-filled day. Every year some 6.7 million tons (6.1 million metric tons) of toxic material—smoke, gas, lead particles, and other contaminants—pour into the atmosphere. Experts say that Mexico City has the world's worst air pollution problem.

How bad is Mexico City's air? Birds regularly fall dead out of the sky after just one flight above the city. Residents keep their windows shut year-round, because if a window is left open, even for a few hours, the furniture will be covered by a layer of grime. During the dry winter months, schools are often closed because the air is considered too dangerous for children to play outdoors. Most Mexico City residents suffer from asthma, other respiratory problems, or eye irritation. Some doctors claim pollution is killing old people and children by the thousands.

In addition to air contamination, the city struggles with a severe water shortage. Seventy-five percent of the capital's water is pumped in from rivers, some of which are as far away as 250 miles (400 kilometers). Nearer rivers have already been drained to dust by the capital's unquenchable thirst. Plans are now being drawn to tap the waters of even more distant rivers, water that is desperately needed for crop irrigation in outlying areas. Mexico City is like a giant sponge, absorbing water from an already dry countryside.

The root of the capital's problems is its huge population. There are simply too many people crowded into the city. Mexico City is almost a country unto itself. The city has more people than Mexico's southern neighbors— Guatemala, Honduras, El Salvador, and Nicaragua— combined. Almost 25 percent of the entire population of Mexico resides in the capital. Mexico City's population began to grow rapidly in the 1960s, when farm people seeking jobs flooded into the city at the rate of 3,000 to 5,000 a day. City services such as providing water and housing could not keep up with the crush of newcomers, and the quality of life plunged for everyone.

The government has designed dozens of programs to ease population pressures and reduce air pollution. Already, car owners are required by law not to drive their vehicles one day a week. To carry out the law, every car owner is issued a sticker that must be displayed on the window. A yellow sticker means the car cannot be driven on Tuesdays, a car with a green sticker cannot be driven on Wednesdays, and so on. Plans are also being made to relocate industries and build new government offices far away from the capital in hopes of drawing people away from the city.

"We must overcome our problems," said the traffic policeman, standing in the middle of the tangled traffic, "or our problems will surely overcome us."

BELOVED TALES

Years ago, folk tales were told from village to village and passed down from one generation to another. Often the stories had a moral, or practical lesson, as in the tale that follows.

"You Reap What You Sow"

Long ago in the dry lands of northern Mexico, an old farmer died. His will divided the family farm into three equal parts, to be given to his three sons. The oldest son was bitter because he wanted the entire farm for himself. The land was of poor quality, and the oldest son believed its yield would be small if divided three ways.

That spring the two younger sons happily began sowing their fields. A stranger with long flowing hair and gentle eyes walked by. "What are you sowing?" asked the stranger. "I'm planting corn," said the youngest son. "You shall reap a good harvest," the stranger said. The stranger then met the second youngest son and asked what he was planting. "Beans," the son said proudly. "Your field will overflow with beans," the stranger said. He then came to the field owned by the oldest son, and asked the same question. "Rocks!" said the oldest son, spitting out the word. "That's all I will ever see in this field, rocks." The stranger nodded and walked away.

When harvest season came, the corn in the youngest son's field was greener and richer than ever before, and his brother harvested a record crop of beans. But the oldest son's field contained only rocks. There seemed to be more rocks covering the ground than ever before. The oldest son sat and wept. Finally he called his brothers to his side. "I have made a terrible mistake," he said between sobs. "I should have been satisfied with whatever our father granted me. And that stranger must have been a messenger from God. He taught me a lesson I'll never forget: You reap what you sow."

The Miracle of Our Lady of Guadalupe

The most widely known and beloved tale in Mexico describes a glorious event that happened soon after the Spaniards conquered the land. All Mexicans hear this story as they are growing up. The tale has special attraction because evidence survives that suggests it is based on truth.

In the year 1531 an Indian farmer named Juan Diego was climbing a hill near Mexico City. Suddenly he heard music that seemed to come from the clouds. Next, a beautiful, dark-skinned woman appeared in front of him. Juan Diego was terrified.

"Do not be afraid, Juan," said the woman. "Go to Mexico City and tell your bishop that I wish a church to be built on this hill so my people may worship."

"Who are you?" asked Juan Diego.

"I am the mother of all who live in this land," the woman replied.

Juan Diego raced to Mexico City to see the bishop. At the time, the bishop was a Spaniard named Juan de Zumarraga. Bishop Zumarraga wanted to believe Juan Diego. It was just ten years after the Spaniards had arrived. Many Spaniards were making slaves of the Indian people and working them to death. The white Europeans believed the dark-skinned Indians were less than human and that mistreating them was not a sin. Now Juan Diego said a dark-skinned woman, who seemed to be an angel, had appeared before him. If true, the bishop reasoned, such an event would surely point out to the Spaniards that the Indian people were their equals in the eyes of God. But Juan Diego had no proof to offer of his miraculous meeting. The bishop asked him to return with some token of evidence.

Juan Diego ran back to the hill, and again the woman appeared to him. She told him to climb to the top of the hill to find the evidence he sought. At the top, Juan discovered a lush bed of roses. Truly the roses must be a special gift from God, because only weeds and cactus grew on the stony hill. Juan Diego gathered the roses and wrapped them inside his tilma, the straw cape most peasants wore. He then hurried back to Mexico City.

Bishop Zumarraga was disappointed. Roses, even those found growing on a dry hill, did not offer spectacular enough proof that Juan had had a divine vision.

"Just wait till you see how red and beautiful the roses are," said Juan. He then opened his tilma, and the roses fell to the floor. Strangely, Bishop Zumarraga did not look at the flowers. Instead, he stared in awe at the inside of Juan's tilma. Painted on the crude straw cloth was a marvelous portrait of the woman Juan claimed to have seen. No one— neither Juan nor the bishop—could explain how the portrait got there.

The Catholic Church recognized Juan Diego's experience as a miracle, but for hundreds of years scholars have puzzled over its details. Many historians believe the bishop commissioned an artist to paint a picture on Juan Diego's tilma and then proclaimed the picture to be a miracle. The scholars say Zumarraga was so desperate to protect the Indians from Spanish cruelty that he was willing to commit fraud. However, other experts argue that no artist in New Spain at the time was professional enough to paint the beautiful portrait found on the straw cape.

The painting now hangs in a golden frame above the altar of the Basilica of Guadalupe. The Basilica was built on the top of the hill in the town of Guadalupe, as the woman

requested. Thousands of people come to see the amazing painting of the woman that Mexicans call Our Lady of Guadalupe. Guides tell tourists that the straw tilma never deteriorates and the picture's colors never fade.

For hundreds of years the angelic woman who visited Juan Diego has been honored in Mexico. Small statues and pictures of Our Lady of Guadalupe are found in nearly every Mexican home. Her pictures are seen in restaurants, above the windshields of buses, and over counters in stores. She is a special saint, loved above all others. And few Mexicans doubt that her appearance long ago to the humble Indian Juan Diego was anything but a miracle.

The old Basilica at Guadalupe

A balloon seller seeks customers.

⑤

VIVA LA FIESTA!

It is a few minutes before eleven o'clock on the evening of September 15 in the town of Dolores Hidalgo. Hundreds of people crowd into the town square. A brass band is poised to play. The crowd senses a feeling of electricity in the air. At eleven o'clock the church bell rings, and the mayor of Dolores Hidalgo appears on the church steps. *"Mexicanos!"* shouts the mayor. *"Viva la independencia!"* ("Long live independence!")

"Viva!" the crowd shouts back.

"Viva Hidalgo!" cries the mayor, in remembrance of the nineteenth-century independence hero, Father Miguel Hidalgo.

"Viva!" echoes the crowd.

"Viva México!" the mayor shouts.

"Viva México! Viva! Viva!"

Fireworks explode, splashing brilliant light across the night sky. The band plays a rousing version of the Mexican national anthem. Church bells peal wildly. People in the square shout "Viva! Viva!" until their throats burn. Even foreign tourists watching the spectacle become instant Mexicans and take up the shout.

The same scene is played out around the country on the night of September 15. It is a joyous re-creation of the moment in 1810 when Father Hidalgo issued his famous *grito* and set Mexicans marching into a war that freed them from 300 years of Spanish rule. The most stirring of all the Independence Day ceremonies takes place in the town of Dolores Hidalgo, where the war for independence began. Following a long-standing tradition, the president of Mexico travels to Dolores Hidalgo in the fifth year of his six-year term to stand on the church steps where Father Hidalgo once stood and issue the *Grito de Hidalgo.*

Mexican Independence Day is also a special day for Mexican Americans. On September 16 (Independence Day is celebrated on the 16th, and the grito ceremony takes place on the evening of the 15th), Mexican Americans raise Mexican flags over their houses and tie banners to their car antennas. Picnics and parades are held in parks all over the United States. It is a time when Mexico's sons and daughters in the United States burst with pride.

Fiesta Magic

Mexican fiestas are explosions of pure joy, unmatched in music, noise, and wild enthusiasm. Often fiestas are celebrated by an entire town. On fiesta days, businesses, schools, traffic, and all other activities come to a halt. The excitement is infectious. Shouts echo off rooftops. At night, people dance for hours on end. A line from one popular fiesta song goes, "Let us dance so that on Judgment Day we will be prepared." The philosopher and author Octavio Paz described the spirit of fiesta in this way:

> *If we hide within ourselves in our daily lives, we discharge ourselves in the whirlwind of the fiesta. It is more than an opening out: we render ourselves open. The somber Mexican, closed up in himself, suddenly explodes, tears open his breast and reveals himself. . . . It [fiesta] fires us into the void; it is a drunken rapture that burns itself out, a pistol shot in the air, a skyrocket.*

The Parade of the Locos is a fiesta celebrated in the state of Guanajuato. *Loco* is the Spanish word for "crazy." Participants in the parade act and dress crazy. Why not? It's Loco Day. A Loco might wear a caveman costume and carry an oversized plastic club. Watch out! He may sneak up and tap you on the head with the club. Mimicking tourists from the United States is a popular sport during the Loco Parade. Some Locos dress as hippies wearing shoulder-length hair, and shirts and trousers ripped to shreds.

Many towns pride themselves on their special fiestas and attract visitors in the process. Carnival in Veracruz, which takes place four days before Lent, is famous throughout the land. During the fiesta, Veracruz residents perform outrageous acts to entertain tourists. One

Day of the Locos parade in the town of San Miguel de Allende

enormously plump man, who normally works as a cabdriver, likes to dress as a beauty queen in a skimpy bikini. He rides in the back of a pickup truck and throws candy and flowers to young men.

Many professions are celebrated with fiesta days in Mexico. On Teachers' Day all students bring a piece of fruit to school as a gift. On Mail Carriers' Day residents leave candy in their mail slots for the mail carrier. On Construction Workers' Day, crews report to their jobs, but instead of working they sit down, drink beer, and sing songs.

Private Celebrations and Religious Holidays

Birthday and saint's day parties are family fiestas cherished by children. A generation ago, most children celebrated their saint's day—the traditional feast day of the saint they were named after. For example, all boys named Juan (the Spanish form of *John*) and girls named Juana would have a saint's day party on June 24, Saint John's Day. In recent years, birthdays have gained importance over saint's days as a time for gift giving and parties.

Both occasions, birthdays and saint's days, call for the grand Mexican custom of breaking a piñata. Practically everyone has seen pictures of Mexican parties with a piñata at center stage. Pictures fail to capture the excitement of the event, however. A piñata is a papier-mâché or pottery figure, usually of a burro. Inside the piñata are candy, toys, fruit, and other treats. At a party, the piñata is hung from a tree limb. One child tries to break it with a club. The other children ring around the action, waiting to dive on the contents of the piñata as soon as they spill to the ground. It sounds simple. But there's a catch. The child swinging the club is blindfolded, and as the child swings at the piñata, an adult pulls the piñata's rope up and down, making it a more difficult target. Breaking the piñata can take a half hour or more. It is a great way to stretch out the fun.

Religious holidays also involve fiestas, although they

are more solemn occasions. The Easter fiesta features a long, slow-moving procession of men and women carrying floats with huge figures of Jesus Christ and the saints. There is no band music, and hardly a word is spoken by the spectators as the images are carried through town. In rural areas the Easter season excites primitive, even frightening passions. Some farm communities carry a papier-mâché statue of Judas to the fields. There the statue is strung up on a tree, cursed at, and finally exploded with fireworks.

December 12 is Guadalupe Day, the day when the miraculous Lady of Guadalupe made her appearance to Juan Diego. On Guadalupe Day, thousands of people flock to the Basilica of Guadalupe to pay homage to Mexico's patron saint. Some walk barefoot, while others drive big cars such as Cadillacs to the church.

Christmas festivities last almost two weeks. The Christmas season begins nine days before Christmas. Reenacting the journey of Mary and Joseph to Bethlehem, family groups walk down the streets of town until they are invited inside by the household that has been designated the *posada*, or inn, for the evening. In the house, the travelers are given food and drink. The ceremony continues for nine nights in nine different posada houses. The posada houses are marked with lighted candles. Gift giving takes place on January 6 at the *Tres Reyes* ("Three Kings") party.

A Good Friday procession

While children at a Tres Reyes party busily unwrap presents, the adults are served a special cake. Concealed in the cake is a small pottery doll. The person who receives the slice with the doll inside is supposed to hold the Tres Reyes party the following year.

Day of the Dead

One day each year is set aside for living people to cheer up the dead. The Day of the Dead is celebrated every November 2. This is the same date that European Catholic countries observe All Souls' Day to remember departed friends and relatives. Festivities in Mexico on this day also honor the dead but have a uniquely Mexican flavor.

On November 1, vendors begin the Day of the Dead activities by setting up stands and selling candies in the shapes of skeletons and skulls. Skulls are seen everywhere. Children wear skull masks, and posters of large skulls are plastered to the walls of grocery stores. In some ways the Mexican Day of the Dead celebrations are like the Halloween holiday in the United States. Children try to scare each other, and playful pictures of ghosts and goblins appear on windows. In the evening, children carry homemade skulls around the town. The skulls are usually fashioned from a shoebox with eyeholes and a mouth cut out. Inside is a glowing candle. The children knock on

The Day of the Dead is celebrated in the cemetery at the grave of a departed loved one.

doors, and instead of "trick or treat?" they ask, "Won't you give something to the skull?"

The morning of November 2 begins with a picnic at an unlikely picnic ground—the town cemetery. Before settling down to their picnic, family groups gather at the grave of a loved one. They clean the resting spot and clear it of weeds. Then they place flowers on the grave. If the departed liked a particular drink, such as cola, someone will put a bottle of it at the head of the grave. Often a family will sing the dead person's favorite song. Finally, baskets are opened, and the picnic starts. Everyone—including, it is hoped, the dead person—has a merry time.

Mother and son fruit sellers on a slow day at the market

6

Mexicans at Home

In Mexico, it is said that no one is ever an orphan. Families tend to be large, so even if a mother and a father die, there is always an older sister, an uncle, an aunt, or a cousin willing to take in the surviving children. A generation ago, families with more than five children were commonplace. Today there is a tendency toward smaller families. Statistics point out that from 1970 to 1990, the average number of children per family has dropped from more than 6 to 2.5. The government supports birth control, even though the Catholic Church opposes the practice. Still, Mexico suffers from an abundance of children. Schools are overflowing. Millions of families live in wretched poverty.

Though families are large, they are also loving—sometimes fiercely so. People outside a family group should be aware that an insult to one family member is considered an insult to all. Bloody family feuds sometimes erupt, especially in rural areas. Despite their passion for protecting one another, Mexican families are remarkably hospitable to visitors. A stranger merely knocking on the door to ask directions might very well be invited to join the family for dinner. When greeting friends, Mexicans use a time-honored expression to tell them to drop in any time: "*Es su casa*" ("It's your house").

Parents teach children to respect their elders and their teachers. Rarely does one encounter a defiant or spoiled child in Mexico. Every family member is expected to pitch in and perform household chores. Usually, the tasks are divided between girls and boys. Younger girls help with the cooking and cleaning, and boys work in the garden or run errands. Looking after babies or toddlers is the job of the older sister. Women's liberation advocates grumble about these arrangements, but they remain facts of life.

Traditionally the father is the family leader. He will announce important decisions to the family, such as the need to sell the house and move to a different side of town. In most cases, however, he comes to conclusions only after long, private discussions with his wife. Moreover, it is the mother whom the children run to with real or imagined hurts. In many ways, the mother's position in the Mexican family is stronger than that of the father.

The role of women in Mexican society is changing rapidly. Just a generation ago, women were thought of as homemakers and mothers, and little else. In poor families, girls either did not go to school or their schooling ended in the fifth grade. Women were not even allowed to vote in all the country's elections until the 1950s. Today, Mexican women serve as governors and senators. Laws forbid discrimination against women in employment and educational opportunities.

Still, old traditions die hard. Some men believe that being an absolute king over their wife and children shows that they are macho. No discussion of Mexican family relations can be complete without touching on machismo. Machismo is a creed that demands super-manly behavior. A macho man never backs down from a fight or shows a hint of fear during a hostile street encounter. Some people claim that machismo has roots deep in Mexican history, when Spaniards pushed aside Indian men and took Indian women. It is said that Mexican men—most of whom have some Indian blood—adopted a macho code as a defense against that historic humiliation. Many men hotly deny they entertain macho feelings. But machismo remains in the background, a shadow that follows men and women throughout their lives.

Cooking

Certain types of ethnic dishes are so scrumptious, so widely popular, they have skipped continents and crossed oceans. Chinese, French, and Italian cuisines all qualify as international favorites. Mexican cooking also falls into that very special category. A traveler will find Mexican restaurants in London, Hong Kong, Berlin, and many other cities in the world.

Despite its popularity, certain misconceptions continue

about Mexican food. For instance, many people think that Mexican food is laced with chilies and other spices, and so is fiery hot to the taste. Not true! The chili, a hot pepper, is closely identified with Mexican food, but it is almost always served as a sauce *separate from* the main dish. That way, diners can spoon as much hot sauce as they want onto their plates. Another misconception stems from geography. Most Mexican restaurants in the United States serve the kind of food developed by Mexicans living in Texas. This cuisine, known as Tex-Mex, is quite tasty, but it is not representative of genuine Mexican cooking. Take, for example, the popular dish enchiladas. Enchiladas served Tex-Mex style are covered with melted cheese. The same dish served south of the border has little if any cheese on top. The spicy stew called chili (short for chili con carne) is strictly a Tex-Mex dish. It is unheard of in Mexico.

Proper Mexican cooking is a fine art that takes years to master. Recipes such as an especially enticing chocolate-flavored *mole* sauce that is served over chicken are passed down in families from generation to generation. Regionalism also influences cooking. In the north a favorite dish is barbecued goat. In the south, broiled fish is served in a spicy tomato sauce. The state of Jalisco is famous for a delicious soup called *pozole*.

The basis of many Mexican dishes is the simple but highly versatile tortilla, a round, thin cake of corn or wheat.

Enchiladas are made from meat or cheese rolled in tortillas, covered with sauce, and baked. A taco is simply a sand-
wich made with a tortilla instead of bread. Here are a few
Mexican dishes that are simple to prepare.

Tacos de Picadillo

Tacos filled with ground beef are called *tacos de
picadillo*. There are dozens of ways to make them. Here is
an easy one.

    1 pound lean ground beef
    1 onion
    4 cloves garlic
    1/2 teaspoon dried thyme
    1 teaspoon oregano
    1 8-ounce can tomato sauce
    1 6-ounce can tomato paste
    1 9-ounce package corn tortillas
    1 small can jalapeño peppers (optional)

Dice the onion and garlic, and fry in a pan with a tiny
bit of oil until soft. Add ground beef. Stir until the beef
is browned. Drain off all excess fat. Add thyme,
oregano, tomato sauce, and tomato paste. Cover and
simmer about ten minutes. Heat the tortillas one by one.
Mexican cooks usually do this by putting the tortillas
directly on the burner of a stove and heating them a few

Tortillas warming up on an open grill

seconds on each side. Spread three or four tablespoons of the meat mixture on a heated tortilla and roll it up.

But wait!

If you are brave, try this variation. Hold a jalapeño pepper in one hand, take a bite of it, and then a bite of your taco. Many people think the way to extinguish the flame of a hot pepper is with water. Wrong! A bite of food taken immediately after a taste of the jalapeño quenches the fiery effect of the pepper and allows you to appreciate it as a spice.

Another hint: Try to buy genuine corn tortillas from your store. Do not buy an item in a cardboard box labeled "Taco Shells."

Licuados

What's the world's best breakfast drink? That's simple. A Mexican *licuado* beats them all. A version of the licuado is sold in some U.S. shops, where they are called fruit smoothies. In Mexico, licuados are also served from stands in the market. They are made from fresh orange juice and fresh fruit, liquefied in a blender. In Spanish a blender is a *licuador*, hence the name *licuado*. Sometimes licuados are made with milk, but orange juice produces a better breakfast drink. The best licuados are made with freshly squeezed orange juice, but you can make this delicious and healthful concoction quickly as follows.

| 1 orange | 1 banana |
| 1 peach | 1 quart commercial orange juice |

Peel an orange, separate it into quarters, and put it in the blender. Add half of a banana and a sliced peach. Fill the blender to the three-quarters level with commercial orange juice and place lid on. Set the blender on high (liquefy) and blend half a minute until the mixture is creamy.

Try other combinations that appeal to you. Use a sliced pear or nectarine instead of a peach, add a few strawberries, or put in a couple of pineapple chunks. Good health!

Liliana Zuniga says "Hi!" from her backyard.

EDUCATION FOR ALL—AT LAST

Liliana Zuniga is 12 years old and a sixth-grade student at the Fray Pedro Degante School in the town of San Miguel de Allende. San Miguel lies in the mountains, about 180 miles (290 kilometers) north of Mexico City. Liliana's teacher is *Maestro Antonio* (Teacher Tony). A male teacher is a *maestro*, a woman teacher is a *maestra*. At Liliana's school, all teachers are referred to as Maestro or Maestra, followed by their first name.

"Maestro Antonio is a good teacher," says Liliana. "He doesn't scold too much, and he doesn't give as much homework as my last teacher." She adds, "My last teacher was mean."

In class, Liliana studies math, history, geography, science, civics, Spanish, English, and religion. English is her favorite subject. Her whole class recently learned to sing "Take Me Out to the Ball Game" in English. One of Liliana's best friends is an American girl, Janna Stein, who lives in Chicago. Every summer, Janna comes to San Miguel with her mother and father for vacation. "I learn more English talking to Janna in the summer than I do in the classroom all year," says Liliana.

Liliana wears a blue and white uniform to school. Nearly all students in the primary grades wear uniforms. Hers must always be washed and pressed, because the category "Personal Appearance" is included on her report card, and she is graded on neatness. Her report-card grades are numbered from 5 to 10. Anything below 6 is failing, and 10 is superior. Liliana gets mostly 9s and 10s. Her classroom routine is somewhat different from most classroom routines in the United States. In her school all students must participate in the *aseo* ("cleanup") toward the end of the day. During the aseo, Liliana and her classmates dust bookcases, and sweep and mop the classroom floor.

In the summers when Janna visits, Liliana compares her schoolwork with her friend's. She is surprised to learn her school is more accelerated than Janna's in the United States. In the sixth grade, Liliana has already begun algebra, something Janna will not begin for another year or two. Children of Mexican farm workers, who spend several months a year north of the border and attend school in both countries, also claim that Mexico's primary schools move at a faster pace. But secondary schools in Mexico are not as demanding as high schools north of the border. Mexico has a high dropout problem, and education leaders try to cram as much material as possible into the primary grades.

Fray Pedro, Liliana's school, is a Catholic school. Her family must pay tuition each month, and the cost is high.

Liliana's classroom at the Fray Pedro Degante school

But there are only 30 students in Liliana's class. Class size in public schools can be as high as 60 or more. Often children in public schools have to share desks and textbooks.

After-School Activities

Classes are dismissed at Fray Pedro every day at 2:30. Liliana usually walks home with her friend Teresa Morales Luna, who is in third grade at the same school. There are no

Liliana (left); her American friend, Janna Stein (the author's daughter); and Teresa Morales Luna

school buses in Mexico. When she gets home, Liliana starts her *tarea* ("homework"). Almost all Mexican schools assign tarea regularly to students. Liliana usually does her homework with Teresa. Sometimes they "play school" and make a game out of the homework. "I'm the teacher," says Liliana, "because I'm older."

When her homework is finished, Teresa, who is nine years old, goes out to play. The street that winds past her house is narrow and paved with cobblestones. Since only a few cars go through, and those that do have to drive slowly, children are free to play in the middle of the street. Teresa plays jump rope to songs that rhyme, but the words make little sense. One jump-rope song goes: *Baila, Josefina/ Como una gelatina.* ("Dance, Josephine,/ Like a plate of Jello.")

Liliana watches the game, laughing. "I'm too old to play that stuff," she says. But Teresa asks her to join. "I can't. Somebody might see me. They'd say I was just a kid."

Liliana looks left and right, a hard, steady stare. Then she bounds into the street and skips rope. *"Baila, Josefina/ Como . . ."*

The Educational System

Liliana attends *primaria*, primary school. Primaria runs from grade one through grade six. After she completes primaria, at age 12, she will graduate to *secundaria*, the equivalent of junior high school. Secundaria covers grades seven, eight, and nine. Next on Liliana's schedule will be *preparatoria*, a four-year program that can be compared to a U.S. high school. After preparatoria, if Liliana maintains good grades and scores high on entrance exams, she will be allowed to go to a university.

Liliana wants to become a teacher when she grows up. She likes the school environment. Not long ago she would have attended a special preparatoria called a normal school to take teacher training. Teachers needed only a high-school education to be certified. But laws were changed in 1984, and now teachers must be university graduates. The new regulations for teacher education have raised the standards in Mexican classrooms.

Mexican law says that all children from ages 6 through 14 must attend school. More than 10 percent of the entire Mexican national budget is spent to support the nation's schools. Still, the benefits of the public-school system fail to reach millions of poor children throughout Mexico today. An estimated one in ten children do not start school at age 6 as required by law. A small percentage of children never go to school at all. The statistics regarding school dropout rates are frightening. Almost half of all children drop out of primaria before completing the sixth grade. This gives Mexico a huge percentage of young workers who have not even completed grade school.

Poverty and years of neglect have combined to frustrate the best efforts of the government to educate the nation's youth. Poor children, especially those in farming areas, grow up among adults who can barely read and write. Many parents, who have completed only a few grades themselves, see little need for their children to have more education. Farm families also need their children's help to tend crops and animals. The children are sent to school when there is a lull in work in the fields, but when planting or harvest time comes, the rural classrooms are empty. Often children simply do not return to school the next time a slowdown occurs in the farm workload. Bringing a sound school system to Mexico has been a long and painful struggle.

Educating the Masses—A Frustrating History

Mexico had no public school system at all until the late 1800s. Before that time the Catholic Church oversaw all of the country's schools. Usually only the rich could afford to educate their children. Although Mexico's President Benito Juárez had wanted to build schools throughout Mexico, his plans were never realized. Nine out of ten Mexican children grew up never learning to read and write.

The aftermath of the Mexican Revolution of 1910–1920 spurred a sudden explosion of energy toward education reforms. The Mexican Constitution, which was written in 1917, guaranteed every child a free public education. In the 1920s a spirited minister of education named José Vasconcelos launched a program to build schools, even in remote areas. Now many towns throughout the country have a José Vasconcelos School, named in honor of this crusading educator.

Despite Vasconcelos's enthusiasm and interest, the government lacked the money to educate all children. Throughout the 1930s, 1940s, and early 1950s, schooling was denied to millions, especially to children from the impoverished farm regions. The scars of this neglect still linger. Today about 15 percent of Mexican adults cannot read or write. Most of the illiterate adults were of school age before the late 1950s and had no opportunity to attend classes.

By the late 1950s the government made a renewed effort to bring the benefits of education to all girls and boys. The thrust has reaped rewards. Enrollment in primary school grew from 3 million in 1950 to 9.2 million in 1970. A government report states that in the mid-1990s, more than 95 percent of Mexico's youth (from the ages of 15 to 29) can read and write. Mexico's public-school system is now hailed as a success.

THE MEXICAN WORLD
OF SPORTS

What is Mexico's favorite team sport? Mexicans will answer in unison, *"Fútbol!"* (what we know as soccer). Even the smallest village has a soccer field, usually near the market or town square. Teams from nearby villages ride buses or walk over mountain trails to play before a small crowd. By contrast, Aztec Stadium in Mexico City, where the professional teams compete, is regularly filled with 50,000 roaring fans.

Once every four years the World Cup Games—the World Series of soccer—take place. When the Mexican national team plays in World Cup competition, a strange tension grips the nation. For weeks before the big game, children chatter about their favorite players. People get into heated discussions about strategy—what grand tactics the Mexican team should use to beat a tough opponent. Though the Mexican team has reached the finals, it has never won a World Cup championship.

The 1994 World Cup Games serve as an example of the spell soccer casts over the country. In a semifinal match, Mexico battled a strong team from Bulgaria. The game and an overtime period ended in a scoreless tie. Meanwhile, city streets were empty. The business of everyday life seemed to come to a halt. All one heard were cheers or anguished moans from people gathered around television sets, watching intently. Then, in a sudden-death shootout, Mexico lost. The crowds swarmed out of restaurants into the streets. And strangely the people celebrated. They sang the national anthem and waved the Mexican flag. Yes, their team had lost, but they had played with pride—pride in Mexico.

Some historians claim the Mexican passion for soccer can be traced to the country's distant past. Long before the Europeans came to the Americas, the Aztecs and other Indian peoples played a game similar to soccer. Teams in Aztec times performed in walled stadiums and moved a hard rubber ball forward by hitting it with their thighs and hips. To the Aztecs, the ball game had a deep religious significance. High priests connected the movement of the ball with the passage of the stars and the moon. Often the captain of the losing team was sacrificed to one of the gods.

Béisbol ("baseball") is the second most popular team sport in Mexico. Over the years several Mexican players have joined the Major Leagues in the United States, and those who achieved stardom north of the border were worshipped at home. In the 1950s a sharp-hitting infielder named Bobby Avila played for the Cleveland Indians. When he retired as a player, he was still so popular in Mexico that the people of the state of Veracruz elected him governor. In the 1970s and 1980s, the left-hander Fernando Valenzuela

Mexico and Norway compete in a 1994 World Cup soccer game.

Basketball players in a city park

pitched for the Los Angeles Dodgers. Valenzuela baffled opposing batters with a screwball that darted in and out of the strike zone. His games were usually carried over Mexican television, and a hush overcame the nation as fans watched Valenzuela's mastery, marveling at his every pitch.

Basketball is also a popular team sport among Mexicans. Outdoor basketball courts stand in all cities and are alive with young players, even in the evening hours. Volleyball, especially women's volleyball, also enjoys a high level of interest. Women's volleyball is played at the preparatoria and university levels, and games are often televised. U.S.-style football (called *fútbol americano*) is also increasing in popularity.

Individual Sports

In central Mexico City there is an aging and dingy sports stadium called Arena México. One night a week it is filled with a noisy crowd of boxing fans who come to watch the last efforts of old boxers and the first fights of new ones. Boxing has a loyal following in most countries, but in Mexico there is a particular drama to it. Fans at the Arena México identify with favorite boxers as if they were friends. They wince when an opponent lands a blow and feel a surge of triumph when their fighter scores a solid jab.

A veteran of the Arena México and of many small-town

rings is Julio César Chávez, a crafty and ferocious Mexican middleweight. By the mid-1900s, Chávez had captured five world titles in three weight divisions and had scored an incredible 75 knockouts. He is adored in Mexico and by Mexican Americans living in the United States. When he fights in the United States, he draws a huge crowd of Mexican Americans, who wave the green, white, and red Mexican flag. Boxing experts praise Chávez as, pound for pound, one of the best boxers ever.

Over the years, Mexican American athletes have become larger-than-life heroes in their native country. Pancho Gonzales was a Mexican American tennis star, born Richard Alonzo Gonzales, in Los Angeles in 1928. With a powerful serve and a slashing backhand, he won the United States Open in 1948 and 1949 and dominated the world of tennis through much of the 1950s and 1960s. Nancy Lopez was born in southern California to a family of golf enthusiasts. By the time she was 11 years old, she was a better golfer than her father. In 1978, 1979, 1985, and 1988 she was named the Professional Golfers' Association (PGA) Player of the Year. Golfer Lee Trevino was born in Dallas, Texas, to poor Mexican immigrant parents. He grew up near a golf course and worked there part time cutting grass. Trevino developed his game and became one of the greatest professional golfers ever. All these Mexican American sports stars are celebrities in Mexico.

Beaches, like this one on Mexico's Pacific coast, give children from seaside regions the opportunity to become strong swimmers.

With thousands of miles of coast on either side of their country, Mexicans have long excelled at water sports. For decades, divers at the beach resorts of Acapulco have thrilled visitors with daring leaps off cliffs into the whitecaps below. Children growing up in the coastal areas learn to swim when they are toddlers, but many children in the dry northern lands never become swimmers.

In recent years, Mexicans have been outstanding in the grueling track-and-field walking events. The 1984 Olympic Games, held in Los Angeles, provided a scene of high drama for Mexican walkers. Race walking is by and large ignored by people in the United States. But in 1984 the huge Mexican American population of Los Angeles lined the streets designated as the racecourse because they knew Mexican walkers were the strongest in the field. And the Mexican walkers gave the fans reason to cheer. Ernesto Canto and Raul Gonzalez finished first and second, respectively, in the 20-kilometer walk. Then, several days later, Raul Gonzalez thrilled the crowd again by finishing first in the very tough 50-kilometer walk.

Among the greatest long-distance runners in the world are Mexico's Tarahumara Indians. The Tarahumaras are a fiercely independent people who live in the rugged mountains in the state of Chihuahua. The Tarahumaras have always been devoted to running. In olden times they hunted deer by running the animals into a state of exhaustion, a feat that took several days. Often the Tarahumaras play a game in which they propel a wooden ball with their feet over distances of 200 miles (322 kilometers) or more. Races among their tribes cover 50 to 100 miles (81 to 161 kilometers). Track coaches watching Tarahumara races marvel at the people's ability and wonder how they might perform in organized long-distance contests, such as marathons. But the Tarahumaras shun travel outside their mountainous homeland and therefore rarely compete in regular track meets. When some Tarahumara runners were told a marathon is about 26 miles (42 kilometers) long, they shook their heads sadly and said, "Too short. Too short."

The Corrida

As the writer Ernest Hemingway once said, "Bullfighting is the only art in which the artist is in danger of death." The bullfight, or *corrida de toros*, was brought to Mexico from Spain. Today bullfighting is practiced in one form or another in practically all Spanish-speaking countries. The true passion for the *corrida* is most intense, however, in Spain and Mexico. Historic bullfighters are idolized. Pictures of such figures as Manolete and El Cordobes of Spain and Carlos Arruza of Mexico hang on walls of restaurants and barbershops.

Starting time for a corrida is generally five o'clock in

the afternoon, when shadows hang over the ring. The pageantry begins with a trumpet fanfare that sets off a colorful parade led by the bullfighters, or matadors, and their assistants. After the parade a gate is swung open, and a huge black bull, usually weighing about 1,000 pounds (454 kilograms), thunders into the ring. First to take the bull's charges with their capes are three assistants called banderilleros. The crowd shouts *Ole!* when the assistant makes a skillful move. Next the picador enters on horseback to jab the bull behind the neck with a long lance. The picador is booed and hissed because his actions weaken the animal. Then the banderilleros return to take turns racing up to the bull and sticking three pairs of wooden staffs with sharpened barbs at the end into the animal's long neck.

The highest moment of drama comes when the matador steps into the ring, armed with a cape and a sword. By this time the bull is maddened by pain and fury and is eager to attack anything that moves. By fluttering his cape, the matador encourages the bull to charge. Waiting till the last instant, the matador whips the cape up and passes it over the animal while its swordlike horns slash menacingly close to his body. An especially brave matador will drop to one knee to take the charge, or he will turn his back to the bull as if he were mindless of danger. When the bull is exhausted, the matador draws his sword to execute the kill. To perform a proper kill, the matador must thrust the

The Corrida de Torros

sword into a spot on the bull's neck that is no larger than a half-dollar. A proper thrust will kill a bull instantly. An inexperienced or unskilled matador will have to stab again and again.

Many foreign tourists watching a corrida will walk out in disgust after the first contest. They claim the spectacle is cruel, sickening, and barbaric. Mexican fans argue that tourists simply do not know enough about the corrida to condemn the practice. The Mexicans say that foreigners see only the blood and ignore the other point, such as the determined dash of the bull and the sweeping moves of the matador. Moreover, Mexicans defend bullfighting as a tradition that is part of their Spanish heritage. The debate over whether the corrida is high drama or plain cruelty continues.

MEXICAN AMERICANS

In the town of Silva, Illinois, a two-block span of road has the unusual name Hero Street. Silva lies in the farm area west of Chicago. Beginning in the 1920s, Mexicans immigrated there to work on the railroad and take jobs in nearby factories. Some families were so poor that they lived in abandoned boxcars.

Over the years the young Mexican American men of Silva marched off to fight. Many won medals for bravery. Eight were killed in battle. In World War II, the Korean War, and the Vietnam War, 78 Mexican American men from one Silva street alone served their country in the military. That is why it is now called Hero Street. Every Veterans Day, groups lay flowers at the memorial that stands at the head of Hero Street, honoring the sons of Mexico who served the United States. These Mexican Americans accepted the duties as well as the privileges of being U.S. citizens.

Four Hundred Years of Immigration

At one time it was fashionable for a select few people in the United States to say, "My ancestors came here on the *Mayflower*." The statement was a boast. Connection with the Pilgrims who arrived at Plymouth Rock in 1620 gave a person special standing as a descendant of the first Europeans to settle in what is now the United States. But long before the *Mayflower* dropped anchor, Mexican priests worked with Indians in what is now the southwestern United States. Settlers followed the priests. In 1610, ten years before the Pilgrims landed at Plymouth Rock, Mexican people founded the town of Santa Fe in what is today New Mexico.

Mexicans were the first non-Indian settlers in the southwestern United States and in California. Pioneers from Mexico established San Antonio, Texas; Albuquerque, New Mexico; Tucson, Arizona; and Los Angeles, California. Some 75,000 Mexicans lived in the vast territories acquired by the United States when the war with Mexico ended, in 1848. Those Mexicans automatically became U.S. citizens.

From the beginning, racial tensions upset relations between the old-line Mexican settlers in California and the Southwest, and newcomers from the eastern states. The easterners were white and Protestant. Often they looked down upon the Mexicans, who were dark-skinned and Catholic. As more and more people from the East arrived, English became the dominant language in the newly acquired territories. Spanish-speaking people were forced to accept a second-class status. Many towns in the Southwest passed laws prohibiting Mexicans from entering restaurants and hotels.

Despite this cruel treatment, Mexican people played a vital role in helping to settle the West. During the California gold rush that began in 1848, Mexican miners taught the "greenhorns" from the East how to extract gold from streams by using a pan. Mexican expertise with range cattle contributed to making Texas a cattle empire. Cowboy words such as *corral* and *rodeo* derive from Spanish words and were first used by Mexican range hands.

Thousands of Mexicans fled their country during the violent revolution of 1910. Most people who left Mexico at that time settled in California and Texas. The revolution destroyed Mexico's economy for years afterward and spurred a still greater wave of immigration. Between 1910 and 1930, more than half a million Mexicans came to the United States. The bracero program in World War II encouraged even more Mexicans to enter the U.S. and work on farms.

Immigration continued in the years after World War II. By then Mexicans had learned the advantages that the country to the north offered: better wages, quality education for their children, and the chance to own their own home. In the United States, newly arriving Mexicans joined an ever-expanding Hispanic population. Today more than 20 million people of Hispanic heritage live in the United States. Sixty-three percent are of Mexican descent.

Illegal Immigrants

It was a broiling hot day in July 1987 when a U.S. border-patrol agent walked passed a boxcar parked at a railroad siding in Texas near the Mexican border. From inside he heard a faint voice crying out in Spanish: "We need help! Help!" The agent turned a crank to open the boxcar's door. He felt a blast of superheated air. It was like opening the door of an oven. In the darkness of the car he witnessed a terrible scene. The naked bodies of 18 young men lay on the floor, their faces twisted in agony. Only one man was alive. He said to the agent, "You've been sent from heaven."

The men in the railroad car were Mexican workers trying to slip across the border illegally to take jobs on Texas farms. Their tragic journey began in Mexico, where they hired a "coyote." *Coyote* is a slang term for a guide, often a Mexican American, who knows how to sneak past border-patrol agents and usher people into the United States. Each of the 19 men paid the coyote about $400 for the one-way trip. He told them to board the boxcar, which was hitched to a train he knew would soon make the crossing into Texas. He then locked the car's door. The boxcar became a coffin as the oxygen inside ran out and the men suffocated, one by one.

Illegal immigrants, often called undocumented workers, regularly enter the United States seeking jobs. Every year the U.S. border patrol arrests more than 1 million undocumented Mexicans crossing the border illegally. Those arrested are sent back to Mexico. There, most simply turn around and head north again. The reason behind their effort is simple: picking cotton on a farm in Texas brings in $6 an *hour*, while the same work on a farm in Mexico brings in only $6 a *day*.

Government leaders in Mexico do nothing to stop Mexicans from crossing the border illegally. The flow of workers to the United States acts as a safety valve for the frustrations of people embittered by poverty in their own country. Many Mexican politicians believe that if the underpaid Mexican workers could not flee north of the border, they might turn to revolution. In fact, wages earned by the undocumented workers in the United States benefit the Mexican economy. Studies show that the vast majority of these workers are young men with wives and children in Mexico. Each year they send an estimated $1 billion home to their families in Mexico. The money from the United Sates is the only source of income for many in farm villages.

U.S. border-patrol agents claim they cannot completely stop the majority of undocumented workers. Guards face a border that is 2,000 miles (3,218 kilometers) long and has countless "weak spots" where people can easily cross. Employers in the United States realize Mexicans are hard workers who are willing to take the kinds of jobs in factories, farms, and restaurants that U.S. workers often refuse to take. Federal laws were passed in the late 1980s to punish U.S. companies that knowingly hired undocumented workers, but the laws have so far done little to reduce the number of undocumented workers coming from Mexico to the United States.

During the 1980s, the United States accepted some 635,000 Mexicans as legal immigrants. This number represents just a small portion of the people who desire U.S. citizenship. Each year millions of Mexicans apply to become legal immigrants, but they face frustrating delays. Many Mexicans simply give up and take their chances crossing the border illegally.

Some Famous Mexican Americans

It was 1884, during the Wild West era, when a group of drunken Texas cowboys rode into the small town of Frisco, New Mexico. The villagers of Frisco were mostly of Mexican descent. The cowboys took an extra swig of whiskey and began shooting up the place. The villagers sent for help. A young Mexican American deputy sheriff named Elfego Baca galloped into town. He arrested one Texan and told the others to go home, but he was soon surrounded by dozens of furious cowhands. What happened next has become the stuff of legend. Baca retreated to a farmhouse, and a 36-hour gunfight broke out. Villagers claimed the Texans fired 4,000 bullets at the house. Baca, undaunted, shot back, killing four cowboys and wounding eight. Finally help arrived, and peace was restored. Baca became a hero who lives forever in the lore of the West. He is an example of one Mexican American who served his community and achieved fame. There are hundreds more such examples.

Henry Cisneros was born to Mexican American parents in San Antonio, Texas. In 1981 he was elected mayor of San Antonio, becoming the first Mexican American mayor of a major U.S. city. Cisneros later served in President Clinton's Cabinet as Secretary of the Department of Housing and Urban Development (HUD). Also from San Antonio is Congressman Henry Gonzalez. In 1961, Gonzalez became the first Texan of Mexican descent to win a seat in the U.S. House of Representatives. Though he championed civil rights, Gonzalez never considered himself to be a representative of minorities. Instead, he insisted he was a U.S. citizen who represented all U.S. citizens in his district.

The 1960s were a turbulent time in the history of the United States. Riots broke out in the cities, and violent demonstrations rocked college campuses. Civil rights and the Vietnam War were burning issues. Folksingers of the period engaged in a gentler, but

Henry Cisneros was elected mayor of San Antonio in 1981.

still effective, form of protest. One of the most eloquent
folksingers of the time was Joan Baez. Baez was born
into a successful Mexican American family. Both her
parents were college teachers. As a child she sang radiantly,
and she mastered the guitar before she was 12. In the 1960s
she became a political activist, marching with Dr. Martin
Luther King, Jr., and giving free concerts to farm
workers. Her recordings, such as the antiwar ballads "With
God on Our Side" and "What Have They Done to the
Rain?" were anthems of the protest movement. Even
some people who disagreed with her politics loved Baez's
golden voice and admired her courage.

Tom Flores, head coach of the Oakland Raiders

Tom Flores was a pro-football quarterback, but he admitted he was not an outstanding athlete. Rather, he succeeded by outworking other players. Perhaps he learned the work ethic from his childhood. He was born in Fresno, California, to a Mexican American farm family. Throughout grade school he worked alongside his parents, picking crops. In the 1960s Flores played quarterback for the Oakland Raiders, the Los Angeles Rams, and the Kansas City Chiefs. Later he became the head coach of the Oakland Raiders. The team was not loaded with "star" players, but under his direction they learned how to outwork the opposition to gain victory. The determined Tom Flores led the Raiders to Super Bowl triumphs in 1981 and 1984.

César Chávez, founder of the United Farm Workers of America

No class of laborers is more poorly paid or suffers worse conditions than migrant farm workers. Migrants travel from farm to farm, working primarily at harvest time. César Chávez knew the trials these farm workers had to face. Growing up in the 1930s, he moved from one farm to another, following the harvests with his Mexican American family. By the time he reached seventh grade he had attended 30 different schools. Determined to better the lives of farm laborers, he founded a union which is today called the United Farm Workers of America (UFW). In 1965 the UFW struck the California grape fields. The strike dragged on for five years. Chávez urged people across the United States to participate in a boycott by refusing to buy California grapes until the farm owners gave migrant workers a decent wage. Finally, the farm owners gave in and awarded the UFW a labor contract. After Chávez died in April 1993, various schools, parks, and streets in the central California farm region were named after him.

The list of extraordinary Mexican Americans is endless. Entire books have been written about the sons and daughters of Mexico who have enriched the United States. These Mexican American success stories prove that the two countries are more than just neighbors. Their histories and their cultures are so intertwined that their peoples are, indeed, family.

APPENDIX ONE:
The Spanish Language

The Spanish language was brought to Mexico and Latin America from Spain. Eighteen Latin American countries claim Spanish as their official language. Mexican Spanish differs only slightly from the language spoken in Spain. For example, a Spaniard will call matches *fósforo*s, while a Mexican will refer to them as *cerillos*. Differences in word usage are small, and anyone who has learned Spanish in Spain or in schools in the United States will be able to carry on a conversation in Mexico *sin problemas* ("without problems").

More than 17 million people in the United States speak Spanish rather than English at home. Spanish is the nation's most widely used second language. More students in the United States study Spanish than any other foreign language.

Common Spanish Expressions

Buenos días. (BWAY nohs DEE ahs) Good morning.

¿Cómo está usted?* (KOH moh es TAH oo STEDH) How are you?

hombre (OHM bray) man

mujer (moo HEHR) woman

muchacho (moo CHAH choh) boy

muchacha (moo CHAH cha) girl

Tengo doce años. (TEHN goh DOH say AHN yohs) I am 12 years old (I have 12 years).

Me llamo . . . (may YAH moh) I am called . . ., or, my name is . . .

sí (see) yes

no (noh) no

por favor (por fah VOR) please

Gracias. (GRAH see ahs) Thank you.

Da nada. (day NAH dah) You're welcome.

No entiendo. (noh en tee EN doh) I don't understand.

¿Dónde está . . .? (DOHN day es TAH) Where is . . .?

¿Qué hora es? (kay OH rah es) What time is it?

¿Cuánto cuesta? (KWAHN toh KWAYS tah) How much does it cost?

Hasta luego. (AHS tah loo AY goh) So long.

Lo siento. (loh see EN toh) I'm sorry.

¿Habla ingles? (AH blah een GLEHS) Do you speak English?

¿Adónde va? (ah DOHN day vah) Where are you going?

¿Cómo se dice . . . en español? (COH moh say DEE say en es pah NYOHL) How do you say . . . in Spanish?

¡Qué bueno! (kay BWAY noh) Great!

*Note that in written Spanish, an upside-down question mark is placed before a question.

APPENDIX TWO:

Mexican Embassies, Consulates, and Tourist Offices in the United States and Canada

In the United States

Atlanta, Georgia
　　Consulate General
　　410 South Tower, CNN Center
　　Atlanta, Georgia 30303-2705
　　(404) 688-3258

Chicago, Illinois
　　Consulate General
　　300 N. Michigan Avenue
　　Chicago, Illinois 60601
　　(312) 855-1380

Houston, Texas
　　Tourist Office
　　2707 North Loop West
　　Houston, Texas 77008
　　(713) 880-5153

Los Angeles, California
　　Tourist Office
　　10100 Santa Monica Boulevard
　　Los Angeles, California 90067
　　(213) 203-8151

New York, New York
Consulate General
8 East 41st Street
New York, New York 10017
(212) 689-0456

Philadelphia, Pennsylvania
Consulate General
215 Fifth Street
Philadelphia, Pennsylvania 19106
(215) 922-4262

Washington, D.C.
Mexican Embassy
1911 Pennsylvania Avenue, N.W.
Washington, D.C. 20006
(202) 728-1600

In Canada

Montréal, Québec
Tourist Office
1 Place Ville Marie
Montréal, Québec
Canada H3B 3M9
(514) 871-1052

Toronto, Ontario
Tourist Office
181 University Avenue
Toronto, Ontario
Canada M5H 3M7
(416) 364-2455

APPENDIX THREE:

Mexican Currency—
The Battered Peso

The basic unit of money in Mexico (you may think of it as the Mexican dollar) is the peso (PAY soh). From the early 1950s until 1976 the peso exchanged at the rate of 12.5 to the U.S. dollar. At that time a working class Mexican family felt secure if the family had 1,000 pesos in the bank. The sum of 1,000 pesos, it was believed, would provide for the family during times of poor health or unemployment.

Then, in 1976, the Mexican government lowered the value of the peso against the dollar. At first the newly cheapened peso traded at 24 to the dollar, but this figure soon zoomed higher. By the late 1980s the peso traded at 3,000 to the dollar. One thousand pesos, the life's savings of an entire family, could no longer buy a candy bar.

In the mid-1990s two types of currency circulated in Mexico: the old peso, which exchanged at 6,000 to the dollar, and the new peso, which exchanged at the rate of 6 to the dollar. The new peso is a simplified version of the old peso, with three zeros taken off. The many years of peso devaluation have caused Mexicans to lose faith in their money. Many people now try to keep their savings in U.S. dollars.

A Time Line of Major Events in Mexican History

B.C.

10,000 Bands of hunters pursue mammoths and other animals in what is now Mexico.

1200   The Olmec civilization develops along the southern Gulf Coast.

A.D.

250   The Mayas begin building their civilization in what is now southern Mexico, Guatemala, and Honduras.

1325   The Aztecs found their capital, Tenochtitlán, where Mexico City stands today.

1519   Spaniards land in Mexico.

1521   Under the leadership of Hernán Cortés, the Spaniards conquer the Aztecs and establish the nation of New Spain.

1531   Juan Diego has miraculous meeting with Our Lady of Guadalupe.

1810   Father Miguel Hidalgo y Castillo launches the Mexican independence movement.

1821   Mexico achieves independence from Spain.

1835   Settlers in Texas declare its independence from Mexico.

1846   War breaks out between Mexico and the United States.

1848   Mexican leaders sign the Treaty of Hidalgo, ending war with the United States; Mexico loses all of its northern lands.

1858   A civil war erupts in Mexico.

1862   The Mexican army defeats a French force in the battle of Puebla.

1863   French troops occupy Mexico and install Ferdinand Maximilian as emperor.

1867   The French are overthrown by the forces of Mexican President Benito Juárez.

1910   The Mexican Revolution begins when farmers and others, led by Pancho Villa and Emiliano Zapata, rebel against the harsh rule of Porfirio Díaz.

1917   The Mexican constitution is written.

1920   Fighting in the revolution subsides, but only after almost 2 million Mexicans die.

1940s Mexican workers enter the United States with temporary permits to work on U.S. farms as part of the bracero program.

1970s Poor crop prices force many farm families to move to the cities, seeking jobs; currency crises cause Mexicans to emigrate to the United States.

1980s Currency crises continue; rival parties compete with the PRI.

1985   Earthquake devastates Mexico City.

1994   The North American Free Trade Agreement NAFTA) is concluded with the United States and Canada. Under terms of the agreement, tariffs are cut, allowing freer trade between the countries of North America.

GLOSSARY

Aztecs—An Indian people who built a civilization centered at Tenochtitlán (the site of Mexico City today) in the 1300s. The Aztec Empire was conquered by the Spaniards under the leadership of Hernán Cortés, in 1521.

banderillero—An assistant in a bullfight who attacks the bull by sticking wooden staffs with sharpened barbs at the end into the animal's neck

Bracero program—An arrangement by which the U.S. government issued temporary permits to Mexican farm laborers to enter the United States to work on U.S. farms during World War II

chilango—An untranslatable and uncomplimentary term used by Mexicans in the countryside to refer to a person from Mexico City

Cinco de Mayo (Fifth of May)—The date of the Mexican army's defeat of a French force in the battle of Puebla, now celebrated as a fiesta day

corrida—Bullfight

coyote—A slang term for a guide, often a Mexican American, who helps Mexicans cross the border illegally into the United States

Day of the Dead—A day set aside each year for living people to cheer up the dead, celebrated on November 2, with family picnics at cemeteries

fiesta—A festival or party for a special occasion. Mexicans hold fiestas for national holidays, religious observances, saints' days and birthdays, and other special events.

Grito de Hidalgo—The cry for revolution issued by Father Miguel Hidalgo y Castillo on September 16, 1810

Hispanic—Relating to the people, speech, or culture of Spain, Portugal, or Latin America (including Mexico)

licuado—A blended fruit drink popular for breakfast in Mexico

machismo—A creed that demands super-manly behavior. Machismo may have roots deep in Mexican history, when Spaniards pushed aside Indian men and took Indian women as wives and girlfriends.

maquiladora—A U.S.-owned factory in Mexico

mariachi—A loud, brassy band typically made up of seven musicians: a singer, two horn players, two violinists, and two guitarists. Mariachi music may have begun in the 1860s, when French troops occupied Mexico and hired bands to play whenever one of the French soldiers married a Mexican woman.

matador—The main bullfighter. The matador kills the bull after a series of skillful moves with cape and sword

Mayas—An Indian people whose civilization thrived in what is now southern Mexico, Guatemala, and Honduras beginning in A.D. 250. The Mayas were the scholars of ancient America, excelling in astronomy.

mestizo—A person of mixed Indian and white European blood

Mexican American—A U.S. citizen of Mexican background

NAFTA—The North American Free Trade Agreement, concluded between the United States, Mexico, and Canada in 1994 to reduce tariffs and promote freer trade among the countries of North America

Olmecs—An Indian people who created the first monumental civilization in the 1200s B.C. in what is now Mexico. The Olmecs lived along the Gulf of Mexico and are famous for their earthen mounds, pyramids, and stone sculptures of heads.

paseo—An informal evening promenade or walk around the town square, enjoyed by Mexicans on Sunday nights

picador—An assistant on horseback in a bullfight who jabs the bull behind the neck with a long lance

piñata—A papier-mâché or pottery figure, usually of a burro, filled with candy, toys, fruit, and other treats. The piñata is hung from a tree limb, and a blindfolded child tries to break it with a club while an adult pulls its rope up and down. The other children ring around, waiting to gather the contents of the piñata as soon as it breaks.

plateau—A high, level surface between mountain ranges. Mexico's central plateau is located between the Sierra Madre East and the Sierra Madre West

posada—An inn. In festivities during the nine days before Christmas in Mexico, families reenact the journey of Mary and Joseph to Bethlehem by walking down the streets of town until they are invited into the household that has been designated as the posada for the evening. Inside they are given food and drink. The ceremony continues for nine nights in nine different posada houses.

preparatoria—A four-year educational program in Mexico that can be compared to high school in the United States

PRI—The Partido Revolucionario Institucional (Institutional Revolutionary Party), a political party in Mexico. Until recently the PRI was the only party in Mexico and thus won all major elections.

primaria—Primary school in Mexico, running from grade one through grade six

ranchero music—Music about the life of cattle ranchers, similar in many ways to the country and western music of the United States

regionalism—An attachment to a certain region of a country or emphasis on characteristics of a particular region

rural—Having to do with the country, country life, or farming

secundaria—The Mexican equivalent of junior high school in the U.S., covering grades seven, eight, and nine

temperate—Mild; not too hot and not too cold

Tex-Mex—Relating to Mexican American cuisine from southern Texas

tortilla—A round, thin cake of corn or wheat that forms the basis of many Mexican dishes

tragafuego—A fire-eater, one of the street entertainers frequently seen in Mexico City

Treaty of Hidalgo—The agreement that ended the 1846–1848 war between Mexico and the United States and gave Mexico's northern lands to the United States

undocumented worker—A person who enters and works in the United States illegally

urban—Having to do with the city or city life

BIBLIOGRAPHY

Fehrenbach, T. R. *Fire and Blood: A History of Mexico.* New York: Macmillan, 1973.

Kandell, Johnathan. *La Capital: The Biography of Mexico City.* New York: Random House, 1986.

Oster, Patrick. *The Mexicans: A Personal Portrait of the People.* New York: William Morrow, 1989.

Parkes, Henry Bamford. *A History of Mexico.* Boston: Houghton Mifflin, 1969.

Paz, Octavio. *The Labyrinth of Solitude.* New York: Grove Press, 1985.

Riding, Alan. *Distant Neighbors.* New York: Random House, 1985.

FOR FURTHER READING

Bierhorst, John. *The Mythology of Mexico and Central America*. New York: William Morrow, 1990.

Brandel, Marc. *An Ear for Danger*. New York: Random House, 1989.

Casagrande, Louis. *A Focus on Mexico*. New York: Lerner, 1987.

Epstein, Sam and Beryl Epstein. *Mexico*. New York: Franklin Watts, 1983.

Pinchot, Jane. *The Mexicans in America*. New York: Lerner, 1989.

Smith, Eileen. *Mexico: Giant of the South*. New York: Dillon, 1983.

Stein, R. Conrad. *Enchantment of the World—Mexico*. Chicago: Childrens Press, 1984.

INDEX

ABOUT THE AUTHOR

R. Conrad Stein was born and grew up in Chicago, Illinois. After serving three years in the U.S. Marine Corps, he attended the University of Illinois and graduated with a degree in history. He later earned an advanced degree from the University of Guanajuato in Mexico. Mr. Stein is a full-time writer who has published more than 80 books for young readers. He lives in Chicago with his wife, Deborah, and their daughter, Janna.

Mexico has long been a second home for the Stein family. The author lived in the Mexican town of San Miguel de Allende from 1973 through 1980. He and his wife and daughter now return to San Miguel for a two-month visit every summer. Vast changes have taken place in Mexico since the author first traveled there more than twenty years ago, but to the Stein family, Mexico remains a land of excitement.